afternoon tea

afternoon tea

Susannah Blake

photography by Martin Brigdale

RYLAND
PETERS
& SMALL

LONDON NEW YORK

First published in the United
Kingdom in 2006
by Ryland Peters & Small
20–21 Jockey's Fields
London WC1R 4BW
www.rylandpeters.com

10 9 8 7 6 5 4 3 2

ISBN-10: 1 84597 205 8
ISBN-13: 978 1 84597 205 9

A CIP record for this book is
available from the British Library.

Printed and bound in China.

Acknowledgements

For Max and Margaret, in memory
of all those afternoon teas
overlooking the Norfolk Broads.

Senior Designer Steve Painter
Commissioning Editor Julia Charles
Editor Rachel Lawrence
Production Eleanor Cant
Art Director Anne-Marie Bulat
Publishing Director Alison Starling

Food Stylist Linda Tubby
Prop Stylist Helen Trent
Indexer Hilary Bird

Notes

- All spoon measurements are
level, unless otherwise specified.
- All eggs are medium, unless
otherwise specified. Uncooked or
partly cooked eggs should not be
served to the very young, the very
old, those with compromised immune
systems or to pregnant women.

contents

tea-time elegance

What I love most about afternoon tea is the ritual and the journey back to a time more elegant and refined than the rushed mug of tea with a biscuit that we know today. A table spread with a cloth and tea (always in a pot) served in cups and saucers. The perfect afternoon tea should begin with savouries – finger sandwiches, little toasts, savoury pastries and other delectable morsels. These should be followed by scones and a selection of fancies and cakes. For a special tea, a glass of champagne may also be served. If you own a set of cake forks and a cake stand, now is the time to bring them out – it's as much about presentation as the tea and cakes.

An array of treats, from mini rarebits and tiny blinis to baby éclairs and delicate tuiles, looks absolutely stunning piled up on cake stands and serving platters. The savoury morsels, delicate fancies and slithers of cake are just a few mouthfuls each, so you can really enjoy the indulgence of trying several different things as you chat over cups of tea.

As a host, there is something unique about afternoon tea. Baking is easy, but the adoration you receive always seems to far outweigh the praise you get for throwing a stupendous dinner party or a show-stopping lunch. There is something about inviting friends or family over for tea that brings out the love.

One of the great things about hosting afternoon tea is that you can do most of the preparation in advance and add the final touches at the last minute, such as filling pastry cases or simply transferring a sticky chocolate cake from a tin to a cake stand.

So with these words in mind, dust off your teapot, put on an apron and invite your loved ones around for an afternoon of refined elegance and culinary delight.

the perfect cup of tea

It seems that everyone has their own secret for making the perfect cup of tea, often one that has been handed down through the generations. The question of whether milk should go in first or second is a subject for fiery debate. For my mother, adding milk first was a definite sign of bad breeding, but for my godfather's wife, the complete opposite. Some people say that adding milk before the tea protects delicate bone china cups from the heat, while others insist that it has a pronounced effect on flavour. For me, drinking the perfect cup of tea should be an occasion and something to stop and linger over. It should be made in a pot and served in thin china teacups with saucers. The brew itself should be one that you can barely taste – not because of a weakness of flavour, but because a perfect balance has been achieved. There should be no thinness or bitterness, just a perfectly rounded flavour. When you take your first sip, it should provide instant comfort and refreshment, and not a single jarring sensation.

The key to making a good cup of tea is, of course, the quality of the tea leaves, and the water. The water should be freshly drawn and boiled (but never reboiled) and the pot must be warmed before you add the tea leaves and water in order to maintain the brewing temperature. The choice of tea is up to you, depending on whether you want a fragrant Darjeeling, a scented Earl Grey, a full-bodied Assam or a smoky Lapsang Souchong. Experiment with different blends and try to choose a tea that will complement the delicacies on offer.

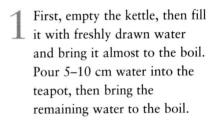

1 First, empty the kettle, then fill it with freshly drawn water and bring it almost to the boil. Pour 5–10 cm water into the teapot, then bring the remaining water to the boil.

2 Swirl the water around the pot to warm it thoroughly, then drain and add the tea leaves (usually a teaspoon per person, plus one for the pot).

3 Pour over the freshly boiled water. Stir once or twice with a spoon, then place the lid on the teapot and brew for 3–5 minutes until the perfect colour and flavour have been achieved. (Do not try to speed up the process by mashing with a spoon – your patience will be rewarded.)

4 Pour the tea into cups using a tea strainer to catch the leaves. Add milk or a thin slice of lemon, or simply enjoy it black. If liked, you may also add sugar to taste.

sandwiches and savouries

Often referred to as Gentleman's Relish, there's something quintessentially English about anchovy relish spread on crisp little toasts. These sophisticated bites make a wonderful start to afternoon tea, especially when served with a light, refreshing cup of Earl Grey or Darjeeling. Leftover relish can be stored in the refrigerator for several days.

little toasts
with anchovy butter

50 g canned anchovy fillets, about 8, drained

60 ml milk

60 g unsalted butter

a pinch of cayenne pepper

a pinch of ground nutmeg

a pinch of ground coriander

¼ teaspoon freshly squeezed lemon juice

8 quails' eggs

4 wafer-thin slices of wholemeal bread

2–3 tablespoons freshly chopped flat leaf parsley

freshly ground black pepper

makes 16

Soak the anchovy fillets in the milk for about 10 minutes.

Drain the anchovy fillets and put them in a food processor with the butter, cayenne pepper, nutmeg, coriander, lemon juice and a good grinding of black pepper. Process until smooth and creamy.

Bring a saucepan of water to the boil, add the quails' eggs, then reduce the heat and simmer for about 4 minutes. Drain, then cover in cold water and let cool.

To serve, peel the eggs and cut in half lengthways. Toast the slices of bread until crisp and golden. Cut off and discard the crusts, then cut into quarters. Spread with a thin layer of anchovy relish, top with half a quail's egg and sprinkle with a little parsley. Serve immediately.

Afternoon tea just isn't afternoon tea without a plate of elegant sandwiches, cut into delicate triangles or slim fingers. From the simplest fillings of cucumber or smoked salmon sandwiched between thin slices of buttered bread to more sophisticated combinations – they really are a must for the tea table.

finger sandwiches

12 thin slices of white or wholemeal bread

butter, at room temperature, for spreading

salt and freshly ground black pepper

Parma ham and fig filling

40 g thinly sliced Parma ham

1 ripe fig

½ teaspoon balsamic vinegar

½ teaspoon olive oil

a handful of rocket leaves

egg and cress filling

2 tablespoons good-quality mayonnaise

½ teaspoon grated lemon zest

2 hard-boiled eggs, cooled, peeled and chopped

a handful of cress

Stilton and pear filling

50 g Stilton cheese, thinly sliced

1 pear

makes 18–24

To make the Parma ham and fig sandwiches, thinly butter 4 slices of bread and fold the ham on top of 2 of them. Cut the fig into thin wedges, remove and discard the skin, then arrange the wedges on top of the ham. Whisk the vinegar and olive oil together in a small bowl, season with salt and pepper and drizzle over the fig. Scatter rocket leaves on top, then top with the remaining slices of buttered bread.

To cut the sandwiches, lay your hand on top of the sandwich and press down gently. Using a serrated knife and a gentle sawing motion, cut off the crusts. Next, cut the sandwich diagonally into quarters or lengthways into 3 fingers.

To make the egg and cress sandwiches, thinly butter 4 slices of bread. Combine the mayonnaise and lemon zest and season with black pepper. Add the hard-boiled eggs and fold together. Divide the mixture between 2 slices of the buttered bread and spread out evenly. Top with cress and the remaining slices of buttered bread, then cut as described above.

To make the Stilton and pear sandwiches, thinly butter 4 slices of bread. Arrange the Stilton over 2 slices of the buttered bread. Slice the pear into thin wedges, remove and discard the core, then arrange on top of the cheese. Season with black pepper, then top with the remaining slices of buttered bread and cut as described above.

Wafer-thin slices of smoked salmon folded on top of buttered wholemeal bread have always been a popular choice for afternoon tea. Topped with a zesty lemon mayonnaise, smoked salmon and asparagus tips, these crisp little crostini add a delicious twist to the more traditional approach.

smoked salmon and asparagus crostini

1 small baguette

12 asparagus tips

2½ tablespoons good-quality mayonnaise

¾ teaspoon grated lemon zest

6–7 drops of Tabasco sauce

75 g smoked salmon, cut into 12 strips

½ lemon, for squeezing

freshly ground black pepper

olive oil, for brushing

a baking sheet

makes 12

Cut 12 thin slices of baguette on the diagonal, about 1 cm, and brush both sides with olive oil. Arrange on a baking sheet and bake in a preheated oven at 190°C (375°F) Gas 5 for about 10 minutes until crisp and golden. Transfer to a wire rack to cool.

Meanwhile, pour about 2 cm water into a frying pan and bring to the boil. Add the asparagus tips and simmer gently for 3–4 minutes until just tender. Drain, refresh under cold water, then pat dry with kitchen paper.

Combine the mayonnaise, lemon zest and Tabasco sauce. Spoon a dollop of the mayonnaise onto each crostini, then top with a strip of smoked salmon and an asparagus tip. Squeeze over a little lemon juice, grind over a little black pepper and serve immediately.

Savoury scones filled with cream cheese and peppery watercress, or topped with sweet juicy grapes, make a wonderful alternative to the classic sweet Scones with Clotted Cream and Strawberry Jam (page 24). They are just a few mouthfuls each, so you'll still have plenty of room for a few cakes and fancies.

baby cheese scones

225 g plain flour

4 teaspoons baking powder

a pinch of salt

¼ teaspoon freshly ground black pepper

50 g unsalted butter, chilled and diced

75 g mature Cheddar cheese, grated

1 egg

100 ml milk

to serve

about 150 g cream cheese

about 40 g watercress or 200 g seedless grapes, halved

a 4-cm biscuit cutter

a baking sheet, greased

makes 16

Put the flour, baking powder, salt and pepper in a food processor and pulse to combine. Add the butter and process for about 20 seconds until the mixture resembles fine breadcrumbs. Transfer to a large bowl and stir in 50 g of the cheese, then make a well in the centre of the mixture.

Beat together the egg and milk in another bowl, reserving 1 tablespoon of the mixture in a separate bowl. Pour most of the remaining liquid into the flour mixture and bring together into a soft dough using a fork. If there are still dry crumbs, add a little more of the liquid. Turn out onto a lightly floured surface and knead very briefly, then gently pat or roll out to about 2 cm thick. Cut out rounds with the biscuit cutter, pressing the trimmings together to make more scones.

Arrange the scones on the prepared baking sheet, spacing them slightly apart. Brush the tops with the reserved egg and milk mixture and sprinkle over the remaining cheese. Bake in a preheated oven at 220°C (425°C) Gas 7 for about 10 minutes until risen and golden. Transfer to a wire rack and let cool.

To serve, split the scones and spread the bottom half with a thick layer of cream cheese, top with watercress, then finish with the scone lid. Alternatively, split the scones, spread each half with cream cheese and top with halved grapes.

Treading the line between a tartlet and a crostini, these bite-sized pastries are perfect for popping into your mouth while chatting over a cup of tea. The contrast between the peppery base, the sweet onions and the salty Parmesan is divine, so you may find it hard to stop at just one.

caramelized onion pastries

1 teaspoon black peppercorns

115 g plain flour

60 g butter, chilled and diced

1 tablespoon water

1½ tablespoons olive oil

1 Spanish onion, halved and thinly sliced

½ teaspoon fresh thyme leaves, plus extra sprigs to garnish

2 tablespoons white wine

1 teaspoon red wine vinegar

1 teaspoon soft brown sugar

15 g Parmesan cheese, shaved

salt and freshly ground black pepper

a 4.5- or 5-cm biscuit cutter

a baking sheet, greased

makes about 20

Crush the peppercorns with a pestle and mortar, then put in a food processor with the flour and a large pinch of salt. Pulse to combine, then add the butter and process for about 20 seconds until the mixture resembles fine breadcrumbs. With the motor running, gradually add the water until the mixture comes together into a dough. If necessary, add a drizzle more water. Press the pastry into a ball, wrap in clingfilm and chill in the refrigerator for about 15 minutes.

Roll out the pastry on a lightly floured surface to about 5 mm thick. Cut out rounds with the biscuit cutter, pressing the trimmings together to make more rounds, and arrange on the prepared baking sheet. Prick with a fork, then bake in a preheated oven at 190°C (375°F) Gas 5 for 12–15 minutes until golden. Transfer to a wire rack to cool.

Meanwhile, heat the olive oil in a non-stick frying pan, then add the onion and gently fry, stirring occasionally, for about 20 minutes. Add the thyme leaves, wine, vinegar and sugar and season with salt and pepper. Increase the heat slightly and cook for a further 10–15 minutes, stirring frequently, until the onion is tender, golden and caramelized.

Spoon the onion on top of the pastry discs, then top with Parmesan shavings, garnish with thyme sprigs and serve.

Traditional Russian blinis are made with a yeasted batter, but these ones are much quicker to make and taste just as good. The salty balls of caviar explode tantalizingly on your tongue and offset the creamy, slightly piquant bite of the wasabi cream. For sheer indulgence, this makes the perfect savoury accompaniment for a champagne tea.

quick blinis
with wasabi cream and caviar

80 ml crème fraîche

¼–½ teaspoon wasabi paste

½ teaspoon grated lemon zest

80 g plain flour

70 g buckwheat flour

1 teaspoon baking powder

a large pinch of salt

1 egg

200 ml milk

25 g butter, melted

2–3 tablespoons caviar or salmon roe

makes about 30

Put the crème fraîche, wasabi paste and lemon zest in a bowl and stir to combine. Cover and chill in the refrigerator while you make the blinis.

Set a griddle or a non-stick frying pan over low heat. Combine the flours, baking powder and salt in a bowl and make a well in the centre. Beat together the egg, milk and melted butter in a separate bowl, then pour into the well and gradually work in the flour using a fork to make a smooth batter.

Lightly grease the griddle using a piece of kitchen paper, then drop small tablespoonfuls of the batter onto the pan. Cook for about 2 minutes until bubbles appear on the surface, then flip over and cook for a further minute or so until golden. Keep warm in a low oven while you cook the remaining blinis in the same way.

To serve, top each blini with about ½ teaspoon of the wasabi cream and about ¼ teaspoon of caviar and serve immediately.

These baby rarebits are real old-fashioned comfort food for an old-fashioned afternoon tea. Topped with jewel-coloured beetroot relish, they make a pretty addition to the tea table. Choose a well-flavoured cheese to fully appreciate the contrast of sweet, sharp and tangy tastes.

baby rarebits
with beetroot and orange relish

1 small baguette

3 tablespoons white wine

100 g mature Cheddar cheese, grated

1 teaspoon Dijon mustard

2 egg yolks

freshly ground black pepper

fresh dill sprigs, to garnish

beetroot and orange relish

1 tablespoon olive oil

1 shallot, finely chopped

1 teaspoon grated fresh ginger

seeds of 2 cardamom pods, crushed

1 beetroot, peeled and grated

¼ cooking apple, peeled, cored and grated

freshly squeezed juice of 1 orange

salt and freshly ground black pepper

makes 12

To make the beetroot and orange relish, heat the olive oil in a frying pan and gently fry the shallot for about 3 minutes. Add the ginger and cardamom seeds and fry for another minute. Add the beetroot, apple and orange juice, and season well with salt and pepper. Cook very gently, stirring frequently, for about 20 minutes until tender and moist, but not wet. Check and adjust the seasoning, if necessary, then set aside.

Cut 12 thin slices of baguette on the diagonal, about 1 cm. Put the wine, cheese and mustard in a small saucepan and heat gently, until the cheese has melted. Season with black pepper, beat in the egg yolks and set aside.

Grill the slices of baguette on one side until golden. Turn over, spoon on the cheese mixture and grill for another 2–3 minutes until golden and bubbling. Transfer to a serving plate, top with the relish, sprinkle with dill sprigs and serve immediately.

scones and teacakes

Traditionally served with clotted cream and rich, fruity jam, these classic scones are a must for the tea table. Originally made in Devon and Cornwall, clotted cream is formed by gently heating milk to produce a really rich, thick cream. However, if you can't get hold of any clotted cream, use whipped cream or extra-thick double cream instead.

scones with clotted cream and strawberry jam

225 g self-raising flour

1 teaspoon baking powder

2 tablespoons caster sugar

50 g unsalted butter, chilled and diced

1 egg

75 ml milk

to serve

clotted cream

good-quality strawberry jam

a 4- or 5-cm biscuit cutter

a baking sheet, greased

makes 10–12

Put the flour, baking powder and sugar in a food processor and pulse to combine. Add the butter and process for about 20 seconds until the mixture resembles fine breadcrumbs. Transfer to a large bowl and make a well in the centre.

Beat together the egg and milk in another bowl, reserving 1 tablespoon of the mixture in a separate bowl. Pour most of the remaining liquid into the flour mixture and bring together into a soft dough using a fork. If there are still dry crumbs, add a little more of the liquid. Turn out onto a lightly floured surface and knead briefly until smooth. Work in a little more flour if the mixture is sticky. Gently pat or roll out the dough to about 2.5 cm thick and cut out rounds using the biscuit cutter, pressing the trimmings together to make more scones.

Arrange the scones on the prepared baking sheet, spacing them slightly apart, and brush the tops with the reserved egg and milk mixture. Bake in a preheated oven at 220°C (425°F) Gas 7 for about 8 minutes until risen and golden. Transfer to a wire rack to cool slightly. Serve warm with clotted cream and strawberry jam.

Crème fraîche and lemon curd make the perfect additions to these light and fruity scones. The tiny chunks of apple in the dough retain a crisp bite, giving the scones a lovely texture and moistness.

apple and sultana scones

225 g plain flour

4 teaspoons baking powder

2 tablespoons caster sugar

50 g unsalted butter, chilled and diced

1 apple, peeled, cored and finely diced

40 g sultanas

1 egg

80 ml milk

to serve

crème fraîche

good-quality lemon curd

a 4- or 5-cm biscuit cutter

a baking sheet, greased

makes about 12

Put the flour, baking powder and sugar in a food processor and pulse to combine. Add the butter and process for about 20 seconds until the mixture resembles fine breadcrumbs. Transfer to a large bowl, stir in the apple and sultanas, then make a well in the centre of the mixture.

Beat together the egg and milk in another bowl, reserving 1 tablespoon of the mixture in a separate bowl. Pour most of the remaining liquid into the flour mixture and bring together into a soft dough using a fork. If there are still dry crumbs, add a little more of the liquid. Turn out onto a lightly floured surface and knead briefly until smooth. Gently pat or roll out to about 2.5 cm thick. Cut out rounds with the biscuit cutter, pressing the trimmings together to make more scones.

Arrange the scones on the prepared baking sheet, spacing them slightly apart. Brush the tops with the reserved egg and milk mixture and bake in preheated oven at 220°C (425°F) Gas 7 for 10–12 minutes until risen and golden. Transfer to a wire rack to cool slightly. Serve warm with crème fraîche and lemon curd.

Zesty orange, sweet and spicy stem ginger and earthy walnuts are a wonderful combination in these little scones. Generous dollops of mascarpone and fig preserve on top complete the effect, creating the perfect balance of richness, creaminess and sweetness.

orange and walnut scones
with mascarpone and fig preserve

225 g self-raising flour

1 teaspoon baking powder

1½ tablespoons caster sugar

½ teaspoon ground ginger

75 g unsalted butter, chilled and diced

grated zest and freshly squeezed juice of 1 unwaxed orange

2 pieces of stem ginger, chopped

40 g walnut pieces

about 2 tablespoons milk, plus extra for brushing

1 egg

to serve

mascarpone

fig preserve

a 4-cm biscuit cutter

a baking sheet, greased

makes 16

Put the flour, baking powder, sugar and ground ginger in a food processor and pulse to combine. Add the butter and process for about 20 seconds until the mixture resembles fine breadcrumbs. Transfer to a large bowl and add the orange zest, stem ginger and walnuts. Combine well with a fork, then make a well in the centre of the mixture.

Pour the orange juice into a measuring jug and add enough milk to make it up to 100 ml, about 2 tablespoons. (Don't worry if the mixture curdles slightly.) Beat in the egg, then pour into the flour mixture, bringing it together into a soft dough using a fork.

Turn out onto a lightly floured surface and knead briefly, working in a little more flour to make a soft, but not sticky dough. Gently pat or roll out to 2–2.5 cm thick and cut out rounds with the biscuit cutter, pressing the trimmings together to make more scones.

Arrange the scones on the prepared baking sheet, spacing them slightly apart, and bake in a preheated oven at 220°C (425°F) Gas 7 for about 10 minutes until risen and golden. Transfer to a wire rack to cool slightly. Serve warm with mascarpone and fig preserve.

These fruity, spiced, spiralled buns have been a traditional English treat since the 18th century. They were first made and sold by the celebrated Chelsea Bun House in Chelsea, west London. Sweet and sticky, and a mini version of the original, these are delicious served fresh from the oven.

baby chelsea buns

450 g strong white bread flour

1 teaspoon salt

50 g caster sugar

a 7-g sachet of easy-blend dried yeast

90 g butter, melted

150 ml milk

2 eggs, beaten

80 g soft brown sugar

1 teaspoon ground cinnamon

75 g sultanas

25 g currants

50 g ready-to-eat dried apricots, chopped

clear honey, for brushing

a 20-cm square cake tin, greased

makes 16

Sift the flour, salt, caster sugar and yeast in a large bowl and make a well in the centre of the mixture. Put 60 g of the butter in a small saucepan with the milk and heat until lukewarm. Remove from the heat, stir in the beaten eggs, then pour into the flour mixture, gradually working it in to make a soft dough. Turn out onto a lightly floured surface and knead for 5–10 minutes until smooth and elastic. Return to the bowl, wrap in a plastic bag and let rise in a warm place for about 1 hour until doubled in size.

Punch down the dough, then divide into 4 equal pieces. Roll out each piece on a lightly floured surface to 12 x 20 cm. Combine the brown sugar, cinnamon and dried fruits in a bowl and toss to mix. Pour the remaining melted butter over the dough, brushing it towards the edges to cover evenly. Sprinkle the fruit mixture on top and roll up tightly from the long edge to make 4 rolls.

Slice each roll into 4 whirls and arrange them in the prepared cake tin so that they are barely touching. Wrap in a plastic bag and let rise in a warm place for about 30 minutes until doubled in size.

Take the cake tin out of the plastic bag and bake the cake in a preheated oven at 200°C (400°F) Gas 6 for about 20 minutes until golden. Brush the buns with honey and bake for another 5 minutes. Let cool in the tin for about 10 minutes, then turn out onto a wire rack and let cool completely. Pull the buns apart to serve.

Made from enriched bread dough, these irresistible little French buns make the perfect alternative to traditional scones. I like them best served warm, broken open and spread with homemade plum jam.

baby brioche buns

300 g strong white bread flour

1 tablespoon caster sugar

½ teaspoon salt

1 teaspoon easy-blend dried yeast

3 eggs

80 ml milk, plus extra for brushing

75 g butter, melted and cooled

5 sugar cubes

sunflower or vegetable oil, for greasing

good-quality plum jam, to serve

a 12-hole muffin tin

makes 12

Sift the flour, sugar, salt and yeast into a large bowl and make a well in the centre of the mixture. Beat the eggs and milk together in another bowl, reserving 1 tablespoon of the mixture in a separate bowl. Stir the butter into the remaining liquid, then pour into the flour mixture and bring together to make a soft dough using a fork. Turn out onto a lightly floured surface and knead for 5–10 minutes, working in a little more flour until the surface becomes smooth and dry. Put the dough in a lightly greased bowl, grease the top of the dough with oil, wrap in a plastic bag and let rise in a warm place for about 1 hour until doubled in size.

Meanwhile, cut out twelve 10-cm squares of greaseproof paper and press into the muffin tin.

Turn the dough out onto a lightly floured surface and knead until firm and elastic. Divide the dough into 12 equal pieces and roll into balls. Place a ball of dough in each section of the muffin tin, wrap the tin in a plastic bag and let rise in a warm place for 20–30 minutes until almost doubled in size.

Gently crush the sugar cubes to make coarse sugar crystals. Brush the tops of the buns with milk, sprinkle with the sugar crystals and bake in a preheated oven at 200°C (400°F) Gas 6 for about 15 minutes until golden and risen, and firm underneath. Transfer to a wire rack to cool slightly. Serve warm with plum jam.

Redolent of childhood, warm drop scones straight from the griddle make a wonderful afternoon treat, particularly in winter when it's cold and crisp outside. This version made with tangy dried blueberries and fragrant lime zest is delicious served dripping with butter and honey.

blueberry and lime drop scones

100 g self-raising flour

2 tablespoons caster sugar

1 egg, beaten

150 ml milk

grated zest of 1 unwaxed lime

60 g dried blueberries

sunflower or vegetable oil, for brushing

to serve

butter

clear honey

makes about 20

Set a large griddle or a non-stick frying pan over low heat. Combine the flour and sugar in a large bowl and make a well in the centre of the mixture. Add the beaten egg and half the milk and gradually work the mixture into the flour to make a smooth batter. Beat in the remaining milk, then fold in the lime zest and blueberries.

Brush the hot griddle with oil, then wipe off any excess using kitchen paper. Drop tablespoonfuls of batter onto the pan and cook for 1–2 minutes until bubbles appear on the surface. Flip over the scones and cook for another 30 seconds to 1 minute until golden. Keep warm in a low oven while you cook the remaining mixture. Serve topped with butter and honey.

Squidgy and spicy, and dripping with melted butter, nothing quite makes a teatime like hot buttered teacakes. These ones are small, rather than the traditional large ones, so there'll be plenty of room for those other tea-time cakes and fancies.

toasted teacakes

225 g strong white bread flour

½ teaspoon salt

1 teaspoon easy-blend dried yeast

1½ tablespoons soft brown sugar

¼ teaspoon freshly grated nutmeg

50 g mixed dried fruits

3 ready-to-eat dried apricots, chopped

40 g butter

120 ml milk, plus extra for brushing

butter, to serve

2 baking sheets, greased

makes 8

Combine the flour, salt, yeast, sugar and nutmeg in a bowl, then sift into a larger bowl. Stir in the dried fruits and make a well in the centre of the mixture.

Melt the butter in a small saucepan, then add the milk and heat until lukewarm. Pour into the flour mixture, gradually working it in to make a soft dough. Turn out onto a lightly floured surface and knead for about 5 minutes until smooth and elastic. Transfer to a bowl, wrap in a plastic bag and let rise in a warm place for about 1 hour until doubled in size.

Turn the dough out onto a lightly floured work surface, punch down and divide into 8 equal pieces. Shape each one into a ball, flatten slightly and arrange on the prepared baking sheets, spacing them slightly apart. Wrap the baking sheets in plastic bags and let rise in a warm place for about 45 minutes until doubled in size.

Brush the teacakes with milk, then bake in a preheated oven at 200°C (400°F) Gas 6 for about 15 minutes until risen and golden, and they sound hollow when tapped. Transfer to a wire rack to cool. To serve, cut the teacakes in half and toast, then spread generously with butter.

fancies

French pâtisserie has a natural home on the tea table, and these baby éclairs give you a perfect excuse to dig out your cake forks. Each one is just a couple of mouthfuls and they look divine piled up on an elegant cake stand.

praline and coffee éclairs

50 g caster sugar

50 g blanched hazelnuts, chopped

75 g plain flour

60 ml milk

60 ml water

50 g butter, diced

a pinch of salt

2 eggs

120 ml whipping cream

coffee icing

25 g unsalted butter

1 teaspoon instant coffee, dissolved in 3 tablespoons boiling water

200 g icing sugar, sifted

3 baking sheets, 1 lightly greased and 2 lined with greaseproof paper

a piping bag fitted with a 1–1.5-cm round nozzle

makes about 20

First make the praline. Heat the sugar in a dry saucepan over medium heat, stirring, for about 5 minutes until dissolved and pale gold. Add the hazelnuts and cook, stirring, for about 1 minute, then pour onto the greased baking sheet and let harden for at least 20 minutes.

Sift the flour onto a sheet of greaseproof paper. Heat the milk, water, butter and salt in a saucepan and bring to the boil for 1 minute. Remove from the heat and, stirring, shoot the flour into the pan. When the mixture becomes smooth, return to the heat, stirring constantly, for about 1 minute. Remove from the heat again and beat in the eggs, one at a time, until the mixture is smooth and glossy.

Spoon the mixture into the piping bag and pipe 5–6 cm fingers of the mixture onto the lined baking sheets. Bake in a preheated oven at 220°C (425°F) Gas 7 for about 12 minutes until golden. Transfer to a wire rack and cut a slit in the side of each one. Let cool completely.

To make the filling, put the hardened praline in a food processor and process briefly to crush. Whip the cream until stiff, then fold in the crushed praline. Using the piping bag, fill the éclairs with the cream.

To make the coffee icing, put the butter and dissolved coffee in a heatproof bowl and set over a saucepan of simmering water until melted. Add the icing sugar and stir for about 4 minutes until smooth and glossy. Spoon the icing over the éclairs immediately and serve.

Filled with smooth, creamy vanilla custard and marinated strawberries, these pastries are simply to die for. They are usually met with gasps of awe and excitement as they appear, swiftly followed by virtual silence with only the squeaking and scraping of cake forks on plates to be heard.

vanilla and strawberry millefeuilles

180 ml single cream

120 ml milk

1 vanilla pod, split lengthways

3 egg yolks

2 tablespoons caster sugar

25 g plain flour

200 g strawberries, hulled and sliced

1½ teaspoons Grand Marnier

¾ teaspoon icing sugar, plus extra for dusting

250 g ready-made puff pastry

2 baking sheets, lightly greased

makes 10

Put the cream, milk and vanilla pod in a saucepan and bring to the boil. Let cool for about 15 minutes. Put the egg yolks and caster sugar in a bowl and whisk for about 2 minutes until pale and creamy, then whisk in the flour.

Remove the vanilla pod from the cream mixture, then pour it into the egg mixture, stirring continuously. Return to the saucepan and heat gently, stirring, for about 2 minutes until thickened. Transfer to a clean bowl and dust with icing sugar. Let cool, then cover and chill in the refrigerator while you prepare the strawberries and pastry.

Put the sliced strawberries in a dish, sprinkle over the Grand Marnier and icing sugar, toss gently and set aside.

Roll out the pastry on a lightly floured surface to about 5 mm thick, then trim it to a 30 x 15 cm rectangle. Slice the pastry into fifteen 6 x 5 cm rectangles and arrange on the prepared baking sheets. Bake in a preheated oven at 200°C (400°F) Gas 6 for 10 minutes until puffed up and golden. Transfer to a wire rack to cool.

To assemble the millefeuilles, cut each pastry rectangle in half crossways using a serrated knife. Arrange 10 of the smaller rectangles on a serving platter. Spread about 1 tablespoon of the custard on top of each one, then top with sliced strawberries and a second pastry rectangle. Repeat with another tablespoonful of custard, more sliced strawberries and a third pastry rectangle. Dust with icing sugar and serve.

Filled with a zesty lemony cream, these irresistible fruit tartlets are incredibly easy to make, but have a certain air of refinement that make them perfect for afternoon tea. Make the pastry cases and lemon cream in advance, prepare the fruit, then put the tartlets together at the last minute.

summer berry tartlets

3 tablespoons ground almonds

100 g plain flour

1 tablespoon caster sugar

50 g butter, chilled and diced

2 tablespoons water

80 ml crème fraîche

1½–2 tablespoons good-quality lemon curd

200 g summer berries, such as strawberries, raspberries, blueberries and redcurrants

icing sugar, to dust (optional)

a 6.5-cm biscuit cutter

a 12-hole tartlet tin, greased

makes 12

Put the almonds, flour and caster sugar in a food processor and pulse to combine. Add the butter and pulse until the mixture resembles fine breadcrumbs. With the motor running, gradually add the water until the mixture comes together into a dough. If necessary, add a drizzle more water. Press into a ball, wrap in clingfilm and chill in the refrigerator for at least 30 minutes.

Roll out the pastry thinly on a lightly floured surface and cut out rounds with the biscuit cutter, pressing the trimmings together to make more rounds. Press the rounds into the prepared tartlet tin and prick the bases with a fork. Bake in a preheated oven at 190°C (375°F) Gas 5 for about 12 minutes until crisp and golden. Transfer to a wire rack to cool.

To serve, fold together the crème fraîche and lemon curd in a small bowl. Put spoonfuls of the mixture in the bottom of each pastry case, top with berries and dust with icing sugar, if liked.

The white chocolate cases are a bit fiddly to make, but the end result of these creamy, luscious mousses is so divine that it's worth every minute of preparation. They are quite rich, so serve alongside a plate of delicate tuiles and perhaps a simple, old-fashioned fruit cake.

dark chocolate, prune and armagnac mousses

140 g white chocolate, melted and cooled, plus extra shavings to decorate

5 ready-to-eat pitted prunes

1 tablespoon Armagnac

2 tablespoons water

60 g dark chocolate (70–80% cocoa solids)

½ tablespoon butter

1½ tablespoons double cream

1 egg, separated

frosted edible flower petals, to decorate (optional)

a thin sheet of perspex

sticky tape

a baking sheet, lined with greaseproof paper

makes 8

Cut out eight 4 x 15 cm strips of perspex, coil each one to make a collar, about 4 cm in diameter, and secure with sticky tape. Stand the collars on the prepared baking sheet.

Using a teaspoon, coat the inside of each collar with the white chocolate, leaving the top ragged and smeared. Drop a spoonful of chocolate into the bottom of each collar and spread out to form a base. Chill for about 15 minutes, then remove from the refrigerator and add a little more chocolate to any thin patches so that there's a good layer of chocolate all round. Return to the refrigerator and chill for at least 30 minutes.

Put the prunes, Armagnac and water in a food processor and blend to make a smooth purée. Put the dark chocolate in a heatproof bowl and set over a saucepan of simmering water until melted. Alternatively, melt the chocolate in a microwave. Remove from the heat and stir in the butter until melted, then stir in the prune purée, cream and egg yolk.

Put the egg white in a clean bowl and whisk to form stiff peaks. Fold a spoonful into the chocolate mixture, then fold in the remaining egg white, one-third at a time. Carefully spoon 1½–2 tablespoons of the mousse into the white chocolate cases and chill in the refrigerator for at least 2 hours.

To serve, carefully remove the sticky tape and unpeel the perspex collars. Arrange on a serving plate using a spatula and decorate with shavings of white chocolate or frosted edible flower petals, if liked.

Macaroons of many varieties can be seen piled high in Parisian pâtisseries, but they are no less out of place on the tea table. Crisp on the outside and chewy in the middle, these little fancies are perfect for balancing on the edge of your saucer.

macaroons

115 g pistachio nuts

115 g icing sugar

2 egg whites

1½ tablespoons mascarpone

15 g dark chocolate, melted and cooled

a piping bag fitted with a 1-cm round nozzle

3 baking sheets, 2 lined with greaseproof paper

makes about 16

Scatter the pistachio nuts on the unlined baking sheet and bake in a preheated oven at 180°C (350°F) Gas 4 for about 3 minutes. Tip into a clean tea towel and rub together to remove the brown papery skins. Put the pistachios and icing sugar in a food processor and process until finely ground.

Put the egg whites in a clean bowl and whisk to form stiff peaks. Sprinkle the pistachio mixture over and gently fold into the mixture. Spoon into the piping bag and pipe 2 cm rounds onto the lined baking sheets, spacing them slightly apart. Transfer to the oven and bake for 10–12 minutes until light golden. Let cool slightly, then carefully remove using a palette knife and transfer to a wire rack to cool completely.

To serve, stir the mascarpone into the chocolate until well blended, then use to sandwich the macaroons together.

Strawberry Macaroons Use 115 g ground almonds instead of the pistachio nuts. Whisk the egg whites to form stiff peaks, then add a few drops of red food colouring and whisk briefly to combine. Sift the ground almonds and sugar over the top, fold in, then pipe the mixture and bake as above. Sandwich the macaroons together with strawberry preserve.

Lemon Macaroons Prepare as for Strawberry Macaroons, but replace the red food colouring with yellow food colouring and add ½ teaspoon grated lemon zest. Mix 1 tablespoon lemon curd with 1 tablespoon mascarpone and use to sandwich the macaroons together.

From dainty pastel-coloured bites to large fluffy clouds sandwiched with cream, meringues have always been a popular offering for afternoon tea. These mouthwatering individual pavlovas, topped with rich cream and fresh fruit, take the humble meringue one step further.

raspberry and nectarine pavlovas

2 egg whites

125 g caster sugar

1 teaspoon cornflour

½ teaspoon white wine vinegar

420 ml crème fraîche

225 g raspberries

1 ripe nectarine, pitted and cut into thin wedges

icing sugar, to dust (optional)

2 baking sheets, lined with greaseproof paper

makes about 14

Put the egg whites in a clean bowl and whisk to form stiff peaks. Sprinkle over a couple of tablespoons of the caster sugar and fold into the mixture. Continue folding in the remaining sugar in the same way, adding the cornflour and vinegar with the last spoonfuls.

Drop heaped tablespoonfuls of the mixture onto the prepared baking sheets, spacing them slightly apart. Using a wet teaspoon, make an indentation in the top of each one. Bake in a preheated oven at 140°C (275°F) Gas 1 for about 45 minutes until dry and just beginning to colour. Using a spatula, carefully remove the meringues from the baking sheets and transfer to a wire rack to cool completely.

To serve, top each meringue with a couple of spoonfuls of crème fraîche, a few raspberries and 1 or 2 slices of nectarine. Dust with icing sugar, if liked, and serve immediately.

Named after the characteristic curved French roof tiles, these crisp, delicate cookies look irresistible balanced on the edge of a bone china saucer. With a light, citrus flavour, they melt in the mouth and make the perfect accompaniment for a cup of scented tea, such as Earl Grey or Lapsang Souchong.

orange and almond tuiles

1 egg white

50 g caster sugar

grated zest of 1 unwaxed orange

25 g butter, melted and cooled

25 g plain flour

2 tablespoons flaked almonds

2 baking sheets, lined with greaseproof paper and lightly greased

makes 14

Put the egg white in a large, clean bowl and whisk to form stiff peaks. Sprinkle over the sugar and orange zest and fold into the mixture. Add half the butter, then sift in half the flour and fold into the mixture. Repeat with the remaining butter and flour.

Working in batches, drop 4 teaspoonfuls of the mixture onto each of the prepared baking sheets, spacing them well apart. Spread out to thin rounds using the back of the teaspoon and sprinkle almonds over the top. Bake in a preheated oven at 190°C (375°F) Gas 5 for about 6 minutes until pale golden. Repeat until you have used all the mixture.

Let cool for a few seconds, then carefully remove using a spatula and drape over a rolling pin, with the almonds on the outside, to shape into curls. Transfer to a wire rack to cool completely, then serve.

These crisp, sticky, chewy cookies typify the elegant kind of morsel that should be served for afternoon tea. They're absolutely perfect when you want to finish with a little something sweet after a plateful of savouries and scones, but when a slice of cake seems just too much.

dark and white chocolate florentines

50 g butter

50 g caster sugar

3 tablespoons double cream

25 g flaked almonds

75 g mixed nuts, such as hazelnuts, walnuts and pistachios, chopped

4 glacé cherries, chopped

50 g mixed glacé fruits, such as citrus peel, apricots, pineapple and angelica, chopped

25 g plain flour

50 g white chocolate

50 g dark chocolate

2 baking sheets, lined with greaseproof paper and well greased

makes about 24

Very gently heat the butter, sugar and cream in a small saucepan, stirring, until melted. Bring to the boil, then remove from the heat and stir in the nuts, glacé fruits and flour until thoroughly mixed. Drop teaspoonfuls of the mixture onto the prepared baking sheets, spacing them well apart.

Bake in a preheated oven at 180°C (350°F) Gas 4 for about 10 minutes until golden, then remove from the oven and gently press back the edges using a palette knife to make neat rounds. Let cool on the baking sheets for about 10 minutes until firm, then carefully peel off the greaseproof paper and, using a spatula, transfer to a wire rack to cool completely.

Break the white chocolate into a heatproof bowl and the dark chocolate into another heatproof bowl. Set the bowl of white chocolate over a saucepan of simmering water until melted, then let cool. Repeat with the bowl of dark chocolate. Alternatively, melt the chocolate in a microwave. Spread half the florentines with white chocolate. Let firm up slightly, then use the tines of a fork to make wavy lines in the chocolate and let set. Coat the remaining florentines in dark chocolate in the same way, then let set before serving.

Thin, crispy and filled with a rich chocolate filling, these indulgent cookies are a wonderful treat to serve with a pot of tea. If you prefer a plainer cookie, however, serve them unfilled and simply dust with sugar or place a few fresh raspberries between each pair of cookies.

chocolate-filled almond cookies

225 g plain flour

50 g ground almonds

a pinch of salt

75 g icing sugar, plus extra for dusting

130 g butter, chilled and diced

1 egg

½ teaspoon vanilla extract

beaten egg, for glazing

chocolate filling

80 g dark chocolate, chopped

80 ml double cream

a 6-cm biscuit cutter

2 baking sheets, lined with greaseproof paper

makes about 15

Put the flour, almonds, salt and icing sugar in a food processor and pulse briefly to combine. Add the butter and pulse until the mixture resembles fine breadcrumbs. Beat together the egg and vanilla extract in a bowl, then, with the food processor running, add it to the flour mixture and process until it starts to come together into a dough. Press into a ball, wrap in clingfilm and chill in the refrigerator for at least 1 hour.

Meanwhile, to make the filling, put the chocolate in a heatproof bowl and set over a saucepan of simmering water until melted. Alternatively, melt the chocolate in a microwave. Stir in the cream and let cool for about 1 hour until it has a thick consistency.

Roll out the dough on a lightly floured surface to about 5 mm thick, then cut out rounds using the biscuit cutter, re-rolling any trimmings to make more cookies. Arrange on the prepared baking sheets, prick with a fork and brush with beaten egg. Bake in a preheated oven at 180°C (350°F) Gas 4 for about 15 minutes until golden brown. Using a spatula, transfer to a wire rack to cool.

Spread half the cookies with the chocolate filling, then sandwich with the remaining cookies. Dust with icing sugar and serve.

cakes

A classic Victoria sandwich filled with cream and fresh fruit makes a wonderful centrepiece for a traditional afternoon tea. Make it in summer when strawberries are in season and at their juicy and fragrant best.

victoria sandwich
with strawberries and cream

180 g butter, at room temperature

180 g caster sugar

3 eggs

180 g self-raising flour

3½ tablespoons good-quality strawberry jam

140 g strawberries, hulled and halved or quartered, depending on size

120 ml whipping cream

icing sugar, for dusting

two 20-cm sandwich tins, greased and base-lined with greaseproof paper

makes one 20-cm cake

Beat together the butter and caster sugar in a large bowl until pale and fluffy. Beat in the eggs one at a time. Sift the flour into the mixture and fold in until thoroughly combined.

Spoon the cake mixture into the prepared tins and spread out evenly using the back of the spoon. Bake in a preheated oven at 180°C (350°F) Gas 4 for 20–25 minutes until golden brown and the sponge springs back when pressed gently with the tips of your fingers. Turn out the cakes onto a wire rack, gently peel off the lining paper and let cool completely.

To serve, slice a thin slither off the top of one of the cakes to create a flat surface. Spread the strawberry jam on top and top with the strawberries. Whip the cream until it stands in soft peaks, then spread on top of the strawberries. Top with the second cake, press down gently and dust with icing sugar.

Perfect for anyone on a gluten- or dairy-free diet, this moist, nutty, tangy cake melts in the mouth and is fabulous as it is or served with an indulgent spoonful or two of crème fraîche. The orange syrup gives it a lovely moist texture.

orange and almond cake

3 large eggs

120 g caster sugar

grated zest of
3 unwaxed oranges

180 g ground almonds

creme fraîche, to serve

orange syrup

freshly squeezed juice
of ½ orange

1 teaspoon freshly squeezed
lemon juice

2 teaspoons caster sugar

*a 20-cm round cake tin, lined
with greaseproof paper*

makes one 20-cm cake

Put the eggs and sugar in a large heatproof bowl and set over a saucepan of gently simmering water, whisking continuously for about 10 minutes until the mixture is pale and thick, and stands in soft peaks.

Remove the bowl from the saucepan and gently fold in the orange zest and ground almonds, one-third at a time, being careful to knock as little air out of the mixture as possible. Pour the mixure into the prepared cake tin and bake in a preheated oven at 180°C (350°F) Gas 4 for about 20 minutes until golden and a skewer inserted in the centre comes out clean. Carefully turn out onto a wire rack, gently peel off the lining paper and let cool completely.

Meanwhile, to make the orange syrup, put the orange juice, lemon juice and sugar in a bowl and stir to combine, then set aside.

Place the cake on a serving plate and prick the top 6–8 times using a skewer, then drizzle the orange syrup over the top. Serve cut into wedges with a dollop of crème fraîche on top.

This tea-time classic feels like a little piece of my childhood. I have countless memories of sitting in the front parlours of great aunts nibbling sandwiches and cakes. Among the many plates that seemed to laden the table, there was always a luscious coffee cake topped with crisp brown walnuts.

coffee and walnut cake

180 g butter, at room temperature

180 g caster sugar

3 eggs

180 g self-raising flour

60 g walnut pieces

2 teaspoons instant coffee, dissolved in 1 tablespoon boiling water

walnut halves, to decorate

coffee frosting

2 tablespoons single cream

2 teaspoons instant coffee

90 g butter, at room temperature

180 g icing sugar

two 20-cm sandwich tins, greased and base-lined with greaseproof paper

makes one 20-cm cake

Beat together the butter and sugar in a large bowl until pale and fluffy, then beat in the eggs one at a time. Sift the flour into the butter mixture and fold in, then fold in the nuts and dissolved coffee. Divide among the prepared sandwich tins and spread out evenly. Bake in a preheated oven at 180°C (350°F) Gas 4 for 20–25 minutes until golden and the sponge springs back when pressed gently with the tips of your fingers. Turn the cakes out onto a wire rack, carefully peel off the lining paper and let cool completely.

To make the coffee frosting, warm the cream and coffee in a small saucepan, stirring until the coffee has dissolved. Pour into a bowl, add the butter and sift the icing sugar into the mixture. Beat together until smooth and creamy.

To serve, slice a thin slither off the top of one of the cakes to create a flat surface. Spread with slightly less than half of the coffee frosting, then place the second cake on top. Spread the remaining frosting on top and decorate with walnut halves.

Sometimes it's the plain cakes that are the best. This one is wonderfully buttery and zesty and is delicious served simply – cut into elegant fingers or squares. To achieve a really crisp, sugary crust on top, combine the sugar and lemon juice at the last minute and pour straight over the cake before letting it cool.

lemon drizzle cake

140 g butter, at room temperature

110 g caster sugar

2 large eggs

grated zest of 1 unwaxed lemon

140 g self-raising flour

topping

4 tablespoons caster sugar

freshly squeezed juice of 1 lemon

a 20-cm loose-bottomed square cake tin, lined with greaseproof paper

makes one 20-cm cake

Beat together the butter and sugar in a bowl until pale and creamy. Beat in the eggs, one at a time, then stir in the lemon zest. Sift the flour into the mixture and fold in until well mixed. Tip the mixture into the prepared cake tin and spread out evenly. Bake in a preheated oven at 180°C (350°F) Gas 4 for about 20 minutes until risen and golden and a skewer inserted in the centre comes out clean.

Transfer the cake tin to a wire rack and prick the top of the cake all over using the skewer. Dust the top of the cake with 1 tablespoon of the sugar for the topping. Quickly combine the remaining sugar and lemon juice in a small bowl and immediately pour over the top of the cake. Let cool in the tin, then carefully unmould to serve.

index